RIVER FOOD CHAINS

Rachel Lynette

Chicago, Illinois

www.heinemannraintree.com
Visit our website to find out
more information about
Heinemann-Raintree books.

To order:
☎ Phone 888-454-2279
🖱 Visit www.heinemannraintree.com
to browse our catalog and order online.

© 2011 Heinemann Library
an imprint of Capstone Global Library, LLC
Chicago, Illinois

Edited by Abby Colich and Andrew Farrow
Designed by Victoria Allen
Illustrated by Words and Publications
Picture research by Mica Brancic
Originated by Capstone Global Library, Ltd.
Printed by China Translation & Printing Services, Ltd.

14 13 12 11 10
10 9 8 7 6 5 4 3 2 1

Library of Congress Cataloging-in-Publication Data
Lynette, Rachel.
   River food chains / Rachel Lynette.
       p. cm. -- (Protecting food chains)
   Includes bibliographical references and index.
   ISBN 978-1-4329-3861-1 (hc) -- ISBN 978-1-4329-3868-0
(pb) 1. Stream ecology--Juvenile literature. 2. Food chains
(Ecology)--Juvenile literature. I. Title.
   QH541.5.S7L97 2011
   577.6'416--dc22
                           2009049552

Acknowledgments
Alamy p. 22 (©jack Thomas); Corbis p. 43; FLPA p. 36 (Tony
Hamblin); Photolibrary pp. 4 (Picture Press/M Delpho),
8 (age fotostock/Michel Renaudeau), 9 (WaterFrame
- Underwater Images/Wolfgang Poelzer), 13 (Animals
Animals/Nigel JH Smith), 14 (age fotostock/Andoni Canela),
15 (Oxford Scientific (OSF)), 17 (WaterFrame - Underwater
Images/Reinhard Dirscherl), 18 (Animals Animals/Victoria
McCormick), 19 (Mauritius/Reinhard Dirscherl), 21 (Oxford
Scientific (OSF)), 23 (Animals Animals/ABPL/M Harvey),
25 (age fotostock/Marevision Marevision), 26 (Robert
Harding Travel/Christian Kober), 27 (Rob Jung), 29 (David
DuChemin), 30 (WaterFrame - Underwater Images/Wolfgang
Poelzer), 35 (age fotostock/Charles Donnezan), 37 (Animals
Animals/CC Lockwood), 38 (Superstock/Richard Durnan),
39 (Claver Carroll), 40 (Ambient Images/Peter Bennett),
41 (Index Stock Imagery/Mark Gibson); Photoshot pp. 33
(©Oceans-Image/Dave Watts), 34 (©All Canada Photos);
Shutterstock p. 42 (Jessie Eldora Robertson).

Cover photograph of an adult brown bear with salmon in
mouth close up reproduced with permission of Photolibrary
(AlaskaStock).

Cover and spread background image reproduced with
permission of Shutterstock (©Patryk Kosmider).

We would like to thank Kenneth Dunton and Dana Sjostrom
for their invaluable help in the preparation of this book.

CONTENTS

Some words are shown in bold, **like this**. You can find out what they mean by looking in the glossary.

WHAT IS A RIVER FOOD CHAIN?

Rivers and streams are full of creatures. All the plants, fish, birds, bears, and beavers living nearby depend on one another for survival. So do all the other living things you cannot see.

Every **organism** that lives in a river obtains its food from a variety of sources, including plants, animals, dead or decaying matter, or **bacteria**. In a river in North America, for example, tiny caddis fly **larvae** eat plantlike organisms called **algae**. Salmon feed on the caddis fly larvae. When a salmon dies, bacteria break down the remains into **nutrients**. The nutrients go back into the river. This supplies **energy** for algae and other plants to grow. Then this process, called a food chain, starts all over again.

All living things depend on one another for survival. All organisms in a food chain need to be protected.

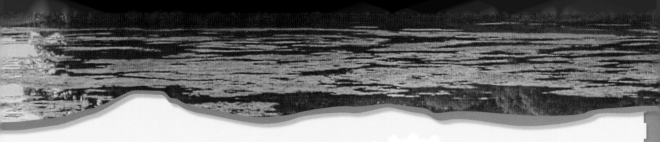

READING A FOOD CHAIN

All organisms need energy to live. When an animal eats a plant or other animal, it gets energy from that organism, just like you get energy when you eat food. A food chain diagram shows this flow of energy. It shows what organisms eat and how energy passes from one organism to another. The arrows in a food chain diagram show how energy moves up the food chain. For example, algae give energy to the caddis fly larvae, the caddis fly larvae give energy to the salmon, and so on.

PROTECTING FOOD CHAINS

Human activity has harmed river **habitats** and the organisms within them. All organisms in a food chain depend on one another. If something happens to one organism, it affects all the other organisms in the food chain. Humans depend on rivers and the organisms in them, too. That is why it is important to protect rivers.

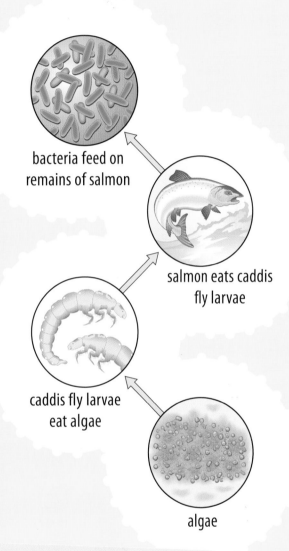

bacteria feed on remains of salmon

salmon eats caddis fly larvae

caddis fly larvae eat algae

algae

A food chain diagram shows the transfer of energy from one organism to another. The arrows show the flow of energy.

LINKS IN THE CHAIN

Each organism has an important role to play in a food chain. Plants are the first link in all food chains. That is because they get their energy from the Sun. Plants convert the Sun's energy into food using a process called **photosynthesis**. Plants are called **producers** because they produce food for other organisms.

The next links in the chain are animals that eat plants. Animals that eat only plants are called **herbivores**. Herbivores are **primary consumers**.

Primary consumers are eaten by **secondary consumers**. Most secondary consumers are **carnivores**, or animals that eat other animals. Animals that eat both plants and animals are called **omnivores**. Omnivores can be primary or secondary consumers.

All plants and animals, even dead ones, contain energy. **Scavengers** feed on dead plants and animals. They also break up this dead matter into smaller pieces for **decomposers** such as bacteria and **fungi**. Decomposers further break down plants and animals in the food chain into nutrients.

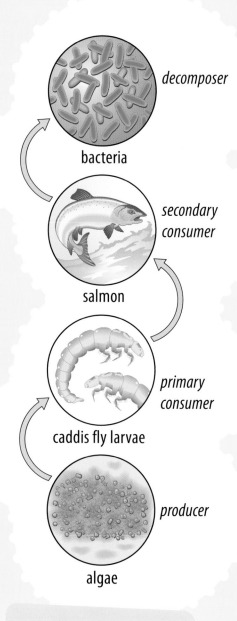

decomposer

bacteria

secondary consumer

salmon

primary consumer

caddis fly larvae

producer

algae

This food chain diagram shows how river organisms are linked.

RIVER FOOD WEBS

Most organisms eat more than one thing. So they are a part of many food chains. Many food chains link together to form a food web. Just as in a food chain, the arrows in a food web diagram show how energy moves from one organism to another.

If an animal ate just one kind of plant, it would be unlikely to survive if that plant were to disappear. But if an animal eats many different kinds of plants, it has a better chance of survival. Strong food webs contain many different organisms.

This diagram shows how the energy flows through a food web.

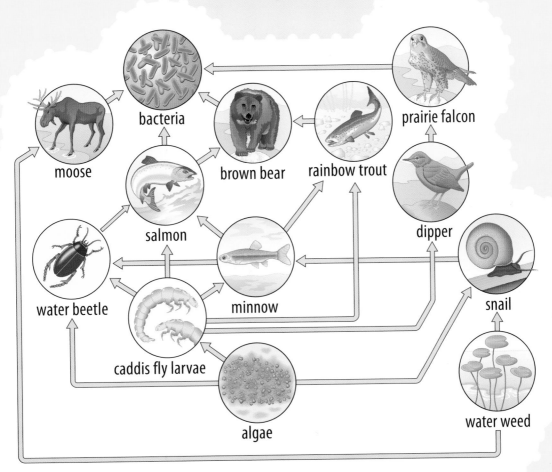

bacteria

prairie falcon

moose

brown bear   rainbow trout

salmon   dipper

water beetle   minnow   snail

caddis fly larvae

algae

water weed

WHAT IS A RIVER HABITAT?

All the plants and animals that live in or near a river are part of the river **habitat**. Some very long rivers flow over thousands of miles. Rivers often start as streams in the mountains. The higher parts of a river flow faster because they are flowing down a steeper slope. The churning water contains more oxygen than calm water. High oxygen levels are good for some kinds of **organisms**.

Rivers end in lakes or in the oceans. The lower part of a river is usually slower and wider. It contains all the **silt** that has been carried downstream. Animals that live in the lower parts of rivers have to deal with murky water. But the water is calmer, so they have an easier time swimming.

South America's Amazon River is home to a huge variety of plants and animals.

These mussels adapt to life in a river by burying themselves in mud.

ADAPTED TO A HABITAT

Organisms that live in rivers are **adapted** to their habitat. An animal that thrives in one part of a river might die in another. For example, freshwater mussels and clams bury themselves in the mud. They could not survive in the faster parts of a river where the mud washes away. Fish that live in the upper parts of rivers must swim almost constantly to keep from being swept downstream. Their bodies need a lot of oxygen. They might not survive in slower parts of the river where the water has less oxygen.

When a river meets the ocean, saltwater and freshwater mix together in an **estuary**. Estuaries are an important habitat for organisms like salmon and eels that live part of their lives in the ocean and part of their lives in freshwater. These animals spend time in **brackish** water to let their bodies adjust to the new environment. Estuaries provide lots of nutrients for plants and animals and are a great habitat for young fish.

WHERE IN THE WORLD ARE RIVER HABITATS?

This map shows some of the main rivers of the world.

NORTH AMERICA

Missouri

Mississippi →

Amazon

SOUTH AMERICA

Yenisei

Angara

EUROPE

Danube

Volga

Rhine

ASIA

Chang Jiang

Ganges

Nile

AFRICA

Congo

AUSTRALIA

Darling

Murray

WHAT ARE THE PRODUCERS IN RIVERS?

All plants are **producers**. They make food. Plants also supply much-needed oxygen to the river **habitat**. They also provide **nutrients** for animals. Nuts and fruits from river trees may fall into the river and become food for river animals. River animals may also eat overhanging leaves.

Most plants cannot grow where there is a strong **current**. **Algae** and mosses, which can cling to rocks, can be found along mountain streams and rivers. As the river gets closer to sea level, the number of different plants increases. In desert **climates**, a river creates an area of lush greenery in the dry and barren desert.

AMAZING ALGAE

Algae are simple, plantlike **organisms**. They live on river bottoms or rocks or just float freely. Often algae look like green sludge. Algae is very important. Most of the world's oxygen comes from algae. Algae are also the base of the river food web. Many small animals, and even some large ones, eat algae.

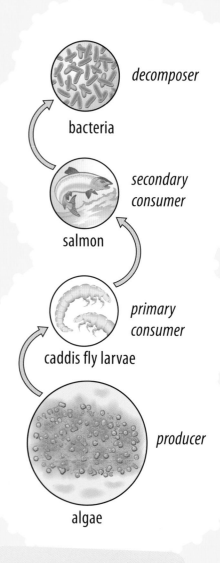

decomposer

bacteria

secondary consumer

salmon

primary consumer

caddis fly larvae

producer

algae

Algae are a producer in a river food chain.

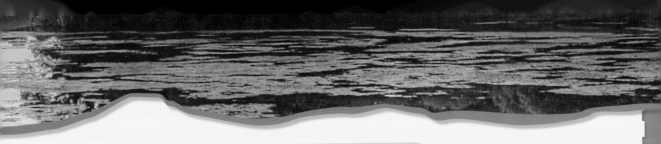

LOSING A LINK: TREES PLEASE

Even though most trees do not grow in rivers, they are still important to the river habitat. The roots of trees growing near a river keep the riverbanks from **eroding**. When people cut down trees, there is nothing to hold the nutrient-rich soil in place. Rain washes the soil into the river. All that soil can clog up the river and make it difficult for animals to survive. Seedlings that are planted on the eroded banks may not grow because all the nutrients have been washed into the river.

Trees must be protected to keep riverbanks from eroding.

FLOATING ON TOP

Some plants, such as lily pads, have flowers and leaves that float on top of the water. The leaves are filled with air and have a waxy coating. This keeps them from becoming waterlogged.

Victoria water lilies are the largest water lilies in the world. They can be found floating on the Amazon River. Their leaves can grow to be over 2.7 meters (9 feet) wide! Lily pads and most other plants that float on water have long stems so that they can take root in the riverbed.

Some plants, such as duckweed, float on top of the water and are not attached to anything. Each duckweed plant has tiny leaves and a few small roots that hang in the water.

Victoria water lilies float on the Amazon River in Bolivia.

Mangrove trees provide shelter and food for many animals in an estuary.

MANGROVE TREES

Mangrove trees have adapted to grow in **estuaries** and other **brackish** water. They have strong roots that can withstand the changing tides. Their roots also filter out the salt in the water. Many animals use mangrove roots for shelter or to lay their eggs.

ABOVE AND BELOW

Reeds and cattails grow in the water near the banks of a river. Their long stems keep them above the water. These plants provide shelter for insects and birds. Some plants, such as eelgrass, grow completely under the water. They must get all of their nutrients from the water.

ALONG THE RIVERBED

Plants that grow along a river provide food and shade for animals in the river. They also help keep the river from getting too hot and the riverbanks from eroding. Berries, nuts, and even baby birds may fall into a river from plants along the bank and become food for river animals.

WHAT ARE THE PRIMARY CONSUMERS IN RIVERS?

The smallest **primary consumers** are microscopic animal **plankton**. They eat **algae** and other plant plankton. Some types of animal plankton are water fleas and water bears.

Plankton is an important food source for many larger animals.

LITTLE LARVAE

Many insects, such as dragonflies, lay their eggs on aquatic plants. Some, such as mosquitoes, lay their eggs floating on the water. When the eggs hatch, **larvae** emerge. Larvae rarely look like the adult insects they will become. They spend most of their time eating. Many insect larvae eat algae by scraping it off rocks and other plants.

OTHER PLANT EATERS

Some kinds of worms live in rivers. They eat algae and pieces of plants that end up in the riverbed. Snails, fresh water mussels, and other **mollusks** eat algae and some kinds of plants. Tadpoles and small fish such as minnows eat plants, too.

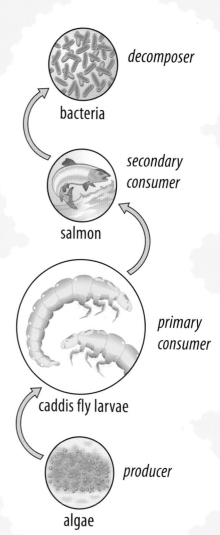

decomposer

bacteria

secondary consumer

salmon

primary consumer

caddis fly larvae

producer

algae

The caddis fly larva is considered a primary consumer because it eats algae, a **producer**.

Some primary consumers do not live in the water. They come to the water for food. Ducks eat aquatic plants. Some ducks are dabblers. Dabblers eat plants that are on or near the surface of the water. Other ducks are divers. Divers can dive down deep into a river to grab plants from the riverbed. Some kinds of river turtles also eat plants.

CADDIS FLY LARVAE

A caddis fly larva has an unusual **adaptation** that helps it build a hard, protective case. It uses a glue-like substance from its own body along with sand, shell pieces, leaves, and twigs to build its case. It takes the case wherever it goes. When it outgrows a case, it must build another. The caddis fly larva seals itself in the last case it builds. Then it changes into its winged adult form.

A caddis fly larva is protected by its tough case.

Beavers make dams from tree branches.

MUSKRATS AND BEAVERS

Muskrats are **native** to North America. Their bodies are covered in two layers of fur to keep them warm. They have long tails that are covered in scales, not fur. Muskrats eat the roots, stems, and buds of cattails, lilies, and other aquatic plants.

Beavers are bigger than muskrats. They eat water lilies, grasses, tree bark, and twigs. Beavers change their surroundings more than any other animal besides humans. They take down trees and build dams across rivers and streams from tree branches and mud. When beavers build a dam, the water behind the dam spreads out into a pond or **wetland** area. This helps the **ecosystem** because wetland **habitats** can support many different **organisms**. Many **endangered species** thrive in wetlands.

LARGE PLANT EATERS

Moose live in northern **climates**. In the spring and early summer, they wade into rivers to eat river grasses, water lilies, bladderwort, and horsetails. Many aquatic plants are rich in sodium, a mineral moose need to survive. Moose are excellent swimmers. They can swim across rivers to find more food.

Manatees live in warm, shallow rivers and **estuaries** in Florida, Central America, and some parts of South America and Africa. They eat over 60 different kinds of plants. Manatees spend most of their time eating.

A Broken Chain: Nonnative Beavers

In the 1940s American beavers were brought to an island in Argentina. People bred them for fur. Over time the business failed. Then they let the beavers free on the island. By the 1990s there were over 100,000 of them! With no natural **predators**, the beavers are destroying the forests at rapid rates.

This manatee must spend most of its time eating.

WHAT ARE THE SECONDARY CONSUMERS IN RIVERS?

Secondary consumers hunt and eat other animals. Most secondary consumers are carnivores, but they also can be omnivores.

SMALL CONSUMERS

Flies, beetles, and dragonflies feed on larvae and other insects. Dragonflies are common in river habitats all over the world. Even though dragonflies have six legs, they cannot walk.

FISH

Most secondary consumers in a river habitat are fish. Some fish, such as young salmon, eat larvae and insects. Other fish, such as adult salmon and largemouth bass, hunt for smaller fish and frogs. Piranhas in the Amazon hunt by hiding behind a rock or plants and waiting for a smaller fish to swim by. When the prey gets close, the piranha darts out and takes a bite. Piranhas usually eat other fish. But a school of very hungry piranhas will attack any animal that strays into the water.

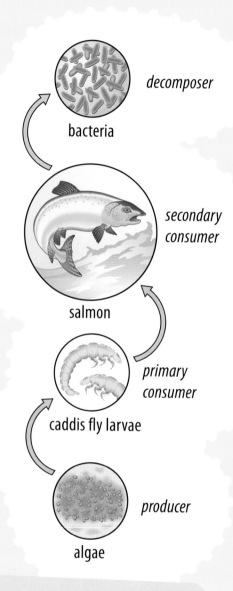

decomposer

bacteria

secondary consumer

salmon

primary consumer

caddis fly larvae

producer

algae

The young salmon, a secondary consumer, eats caddis fly larvae.

SHARP-SHOOTING ARCHERFISH

Archerfish live in rivers, streams, and **estuaries** across Asia and Australia. Archerfish hunt by spitting a stream of water at insects on branches hanging above the water. They can hit a target more than 1.5 meters (5 feet) away! When an archerfish hits an insect, the prey falls into the water. Then the archerfish devours it.

BIRDS OF PREY

Many kinds of birds come to rivers to hunt. Large birds such as herons and egrets stand still in the water and wait for fish to swim close. Then they grab them with their large beaks. Kingfishers perch in trees near rivers and swoop down to catch fish. Eagles and osprey soar overhead looking for fish near the surface. Then they swoop down and grab the fish with their **talons**.

The archerfish knocks insects into the water by shooting water at them.

AMPHIBIANS

Frogs catch insects with their quick, long tongues. Most salamanders prey on slow-moving animals such as worms, slugs, and snails. Some salamanders and frogs are poisonous. They are brightly colored, and larger animals know not to eat them. Their bright colors scare off many **predators**.

This green frog attacks a dragonfly.

MAMMALS

Mammals that live in and near rivers may prey on insects, fish, and amphibians. Freshwater dolphins live in some **tropical** rivers. They have poor eyesight and use **echolocation** to find their prey in murky water. River otters have long, sleek bodies with webbed feet and sharp claws. River otters eat mostly fish and will hunt for three or four hours a day. When they are not hunting, they play in the water.

Raccoons and bears are omnivores. They come to rivers to hunt. Raccoons eat frogs and crayfish. Bears wade into the water to hunt for salmon as they swim upstream to **spawn**.

This crocodile has caught a meal.

LARGE REPTILES

The alligator snapping turtle is one of the biggest freshwater turtles. It lives in North American rivers and eats minnows and other small fish. In warmer **climates**, crocodiles are at the top of the food chain. A crocodile can stay very still for a long time. Then it will suddenly snap at another animal that has come too close!

LOSING A LINK: DISAPPEARING FROGS

Frogs and toads have been disappearing worldwide. One-third of the more than 6,000 **species** are now at risk of dying out. Human activities are partly to blame. Scientists also think a highly **contagious fungus** is causing disease in many frogs. Frogs are an important link in the food chain. They eat large amounts of insects and are an important food source for other **consumers**.

WHAT ARE THE DECOMPOSERS IN RIVERS?

When plants and animals die, **scavengers** and **decomposers** consume the remains. Without these important **organisms**, the rivers would be filled with dead plants and animals.

SCAVENGERS

Scavengers look for dead plants and animals to eat. Sometimes they find an animal that has died. Other times they eat parts of dead plants and animals that other animals have left behind.

Many scavengers live in the sand or mud at the bottom of a river. This is a good place to find food. When a organism dies, it often sinks.

Scavengers such as crayfish and some kinds of catfish are **omnivores**. They eat dead plant and animal matter. Other scavengers are **herbivores** that eat only plants. Snails and freshwater crabs eat rotting plants. Flatworms can sense rotting flesh. They have long feeding tubes that suck up dead plant and animal matter.

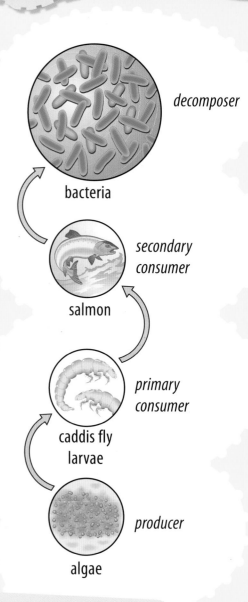

decomposer

bacteria

secondary consumer

salmon

primary consumer

caddis fly larvae

producer

algae

Bacteria break down dead organisms at all levels of the food chain.

These crayfish are feasting on a dead carp.

Piranhas are important scavengers in the Amazon. Besides fruit and live animals, piranhas consume dead animals. Sometimes they eat fish or other river animals. Sometimes they feed on a large animal, such as a tapir or cow, that has died in the water.

PROTECTING A LINK: ENDANGERED CRABS

Many scientists are concerned about **endangered** freshwater crabs. The crabs play an important part in the **ecosystem**. They help return **nutrients** to rivers by scavenging for dead plants and animals. They are also a source of food for many larger animals. Freshwater crabs need clean water to live. When the water is **polluted**, the number of crabs goes down. When people clean up a polluted river, they help the freshwater crabs!

This delta is rich in plant life because so many nutrients have been washed downstream.

BACTERIA AND FUNGI

Bacteria and **fungi** are decomposers. They feed on dead plants and animals. Sometimes they feed on the parts that scavengers have left behind. Decomposers use some of what they eat for **energy**. The rest breaks down into nutrients such as **nitrate**, an important nutrient for plants. Without decomposers, Earth would run out of nutrients, and plants would not be able to grow. Because they feed on all organisms, decomposers are a part of each level in a food chain.

When decomposers break down plant and animal matter, some of the nutrients fall to the river bottom. There they are used by plants. In rivers with fast **currents**, the nutrients may be swept many miles downstream. They may end up in a calm, muddy part of the river. All those nutrients help many different kinds of plants grow in that part of the river. The plants will attract the **primary consumers** that eat them. Those animals will attract **secondary consumers**. All those plants and animals create strong food chains and a thriving ecosystem. None of this would be possible without the nutrients that come from decomposing plants and animals.

A BROKEN CHAIN: NOT ENOUGH OXYGEN

Farmers use **fertilizers** to make their crops grow faster and bigger. Some of the fertilizer runs off into nearby rivers. The nutrients from fertilizer can cause too much **algae** to grow, called an algae bloom. When the algae die, bacteria work to break them down. However, it takes a great deal of bacteria to decompose all that algae. The bacteria use all the oxygen in the environment. Other animals may die because they cannot get enough oxygen.

The bacteria that consume algae from algae blooms, such as this one, take up oxygen from other organisms and harm river food chains.

WHAT ARE RIVER FOOD CHAINS LIKE AROUND THE WORLD?

Different rivers have different food chains. So do different parts of the same river. The **climate**, the speed of the **currents**, and human activity around the river all affect what kinds of **organisms** live there.

THE MISSISSIPPI RIVER

The Mississippi River begins at Lake Itasca in northern Minnesota. It ends where it meets the Gulf of Mexico. The lower part of the Mississippi runs more slowly. The Mississippi often floods its banks, creating **wetlands**.

Plant life thrives in the slow-moving Mississippi. Many small animals live among the plants, including insects, snails, and tadpoles. Crayfish **prey** on these animals, as well as on dead plants and animals. Crayfish are eaten by mudpuppies, a type of salamander. Mudpuppies can grow up to 40 centimeters (16 inches) long and live their entire lives underwater. Mudpuppies are eaten by blue catfish. The catfish, in turn, are eaten by blue herons.

This food chain shows how these four Mississippi River organisms are connected.

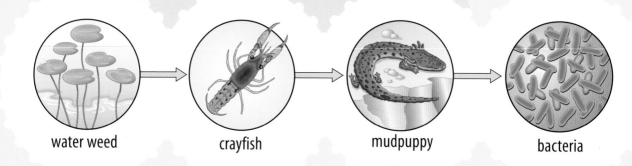

water weed   crayfish   mudpuppy   bacteria

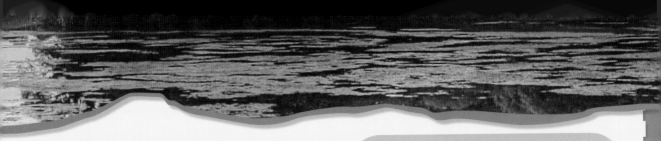

THE GANGES RIVER

The Ganges River in India is one of the most **polluted** rivers in the world. Raw sewage, **fertilizers**, and factory waste flow directly into the river. In many places, the river is not safe for drinking or even bathing. Most animals cannot survive in such a polluted river. Many **species** of fish have simply disappeared from the Ganges.

SMALL CHANGES, BIG RESULTS

Changes have taken place at the small village of Raja Karna on the Ganges River. People there have learned how to make their own **organic** (natural) fertilizer. They know how to treat the waste to make it safer. The number of **endangered** freshwater dolphins has doubled in that part of the river. The water is now safer to drink.

Thousands of people bathe in the Ganges River, even though it is very polluted.

Nonnative zebra mussels multiply quickly in the Thames River.

THE THAMES RIVER

The Thames River is the second-largest river in the United Kingdom. It runs through southern England into the North Sea. Many kinds of fish, birds, and other animals live in the Thames. But some animals that live there should not be there.

Several types of **nonnative** shellfish got to the Thames on the hulls of cargo ships. Zebra mussels and Asiatic clams multiply quickly. They compete with **native** species for food and space. Chinese mitten crabs are fierce **predators**. They often take food from native species. They also burrow into the riverbank, causing **erosion**. Some people think the best way to control these crabs is to eat them! Mitten crabs are seen as a tasty treat in some parts of Asia. Why do you think nonnative species are harmful to native food chains?

THE AMAZON RIVER

The Amazon River **basin** in South America is home to more organisms than anywhere else in the world. Each year during the rainy season, the Amazon floods its banks. The flooding water brings **nutrients** to plants and animals for miles around.

The Amazon is home to more than 3,000 different kinds of fish. Beautiful angelfish eat daphnia, a type of **plankton**. Angelfish are eaten by piranhas. Even the fierce piranha has predators. Piranhas may be eaten by bigger fish, turtles, otters, or even other piranhas!

LOSING A LINK: THE PINK DOLPHIN

The pink dolphin is a freshwater dolphin that lives in the Amazon. It is on the brink of extinction (dying out). Pink dolphins help keep fish populations down. They eat small fish such as catfish and shellfish. **Habitat** destruction, mercury **pollution** from gold mines, and accidents with fishing nets and boats have killed off many dolphins. Today, this smart, friendly animal is considered vulnerable.

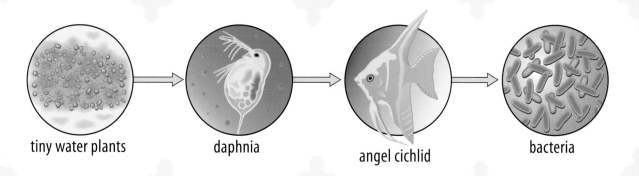

tiny water plants   daphnia   angel cichlid   bacteria

This is a food chain from the Amazon River.

THE NILE RIVER

The Nile is the longest river in the world. It stretches 6,650 kilometers (4,132 miles) from mountains in South Africa to the Mediterranean Sea. Tall papaya reeds grow in some parts of the river. Their thick roots create swamps that support many plants and animals. Small fish hide among the reeds. These fish become food for kingfishers and other predators. A type of catfish swims upside-down to feed on plants floating on the river's surface. Catfish and other fish get snapped up by crocodiles.

A BROKEN CHAIN: NO MORE FLOODING

The Aswan Dam was completed in 1970. It stopped the Nile from flooding during the yearly rainy season. The flooding brought nutrients to the land around the Nile. Now farmers use fertilizers to replace the missing nutrients. The fertilizers leach into the river. They pollute the habitat for the plants and animals that live there.

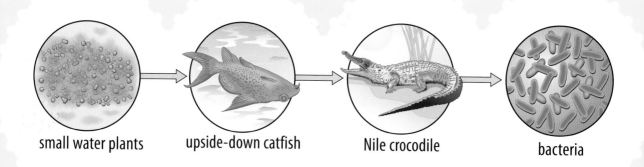

small water plants   upside-down catfish   Nile crocodile   bacteria

This food chain shows how **energy** flows from one Nile River organism to another.

This female platypus swims underwater in Australia.

THE MURRAY RIVER

The Murray River begins in the Australian Alps. It runs through southern Australia and drains into the Indian Ocean. The river is rich in wildlife. But pollution is causing some species to decline in numbers. The Murray River was once home to many platypuses. Because of pollution, their food sources have declined, which has caused them to decline. Now they live only in some parts of the river.

Platypuses are native to Australia and nowhere else. They are one of only two kinds of **mammals** that lay eggs. A platypus must eat 15 to 30 percent of its body weight each day. This means it must spend most of its time hunting. Platypuses eat insects, shellfish, crayfish, and other small prey. When hunting, a platypus fills up its cheek pouches with prey underwater. Then it swims to the surface to chew its catch.

HOW ARE HUMANS HARMING RIVER FOOD CHAINS?

Many things can damage a food chain. Sometimes a natural cause upsets a food chain. It might be a disease that attacks a specific **species**. Or it can be a flood, earthquake, or other natural disaster that changes the **ecosystem**. Humans have done much more damage to food chains than nature. Over time humans have affected food chains all over the world.

HABITAT LOSS

Habitat loss is the biggest threat to river food chains. When people cut down trees, they destroy animal homes and food sources. Beavers need trees to build their dams and lodges. Many species of fish eat leaves and fruit that fall into the river. Without trees there are no leaves or fruit for them to eat. Cutting down trees by a river also takes away shade. This can make the river warmer. Cold-water fish such as salmon cannot live in warm water.

This photo shows the damage clear-cut logging can cause on a river in Canada.

34

POLLUTION

Humans also harm food chains with **pollution**. Farming, mining, and other activities use poisonous chemicals that end up in rivers. Many animals cannot live in a **polluted** habitat. The Yangtze in China and the Ganges in India are very polluted rivers. Animals that used to be plentiful in those rivers are now **endangered** or **extinct** (died out). One sad example is the baiji, a freshwater dolphin that lived in the Yangtze. The baiji were suspected to have become extinct in 2007.

A BROKEN CHAIN: FRASER RIVER ESTUARY

Habitat loss has had a major effect on the Fraser River **Estuary** in British Columbia, Canada. The estuary is home to endangered species of salmon and sturgeon. Millions of birds rest there while **migrating** from the Arctic to South America.

Humans cause large amounts of river pollution.

DAMS

People build dams on rivers to control flooding, **irrigate** land, and produce **hydroelectricity**. There are more than 40,000 large dams in the world. Often a big river has many dams.

Damming a river changes the ecosystem and disrupts food chains. **Nutrients** and **silt** end up behind the dam and do not flow downstream. Without silt, the riverbed below the dam becomes rocky. Plants cannot grow there. Animals that burrow into muddy river bottoms, such as clams and mussels, lose their habitat. Dams also block migrating fish such as salmon and eels. If salmon cannot make it upstream, they cannot **spawn**. Then no new salmon are produced.

This photo shows an Atlantic salmon trapped by a dam.

This river is full of hydrillas from India.

ALIEN SPECIES

Alien, or **nonnative**, plants and animals are a problem in rivers all over the world. A plant or animal that is an important part of the food chain in its natural habitat can cause many problems if it ends up somewhere else.

Nonnative species may breed quickly and damage an entire habitat. Often nonnative plants are not eaten or used by **native** animals. Nonnative plants can cover an area of a river. They make it impossible for other plants to grow and for animals to live there. Nonnative animals usually do not have any natural **predators**. Nonnative animals compete with native ones for food and for space.

INVASIVE SPECIES: HYDRILLA

Hydrillas are underwater plants native to Asia, Europe, and Australia. Pet stores in the United States sold them for people to put in fish tanks. Some of these owners dumped their aquariums into rivers. The plants spread quickly and formed thick mats. This makes it difficult for fish and other native animals to live there.

Camping near a river can be fun, but try not to trample plants or damage other river **organisms**.

PEOPLE ON THE RIVER

Many people enjoy spending time near rivers. People camp, swim, boat, fish, and hunt there. But these activities can damage habitats and disrupt food chains. People often trample plants and frighten wildlife near rivers. Sometimes people leave behind litter. Propellers on motor boats can harm or even kill aquatic animals such as freshwater dolphins and manatees. Large ships also crash into these animals.

Fishing and hunting also cause problems. Overfishing leads to fewer fish for bigger predators to eat. Salmon are often overfished. Animals that live near the river are also in danger. In England beavers were once hunted for their fur but became extinct in the 1400s.

CLIMATE CHANGE

Scientists believe that human activity is causing temperatures to rise around the world. Warmer temperatures reduce the amount of water in rivers. Scientists worry that large rivers such as the Ganges, Yellow, and Niger could dry up completely. Without these rivers many animals would die. Some species could become extinct.

Climate change also can make the water too warm for cold-water species. If a species cannot **adapt**, it will be in danger of becoming extinct. Warmer water might also help nonnative species, such as zebra mussels, breed faster. Also, warmer water might attract more mosquitoes. Mosquitoes can carry dangerous diseases such as malaria, yellow fever, and West Nile virus.

A Broken Chain: Water Shortage

People rely on river water for drinking, farming, and hydroelectricity. Reduced water flow in major rivers means there might not be enough for people. This is especially a problem in poorer countries.

Climate change is causing rivers to dry up all over the world.

WHAT CAN YOU DO TO PROTECT RIVER FOOD CHAINS?

Rivers are not just important to fish and animals. They are important to people, too! Many people use rivers for drinking, bathing, and washing clothes. People also use rivers for boating and for moving goods from one place to another. That is why people often build cities near rivers. Farmers use river water to **irrigate** their crops. People also eat fish and other animals that live in rivers.

There are many ways people can help protect rivers. Scientists study rivers to learn more about the plants and animals that live there. They also find out what plants and animals are **endangered**. **Conservation** groups work to save endangered **species** and to clean up **polluted** rivers.

These people are helping the river habitat by cleaning up litter.

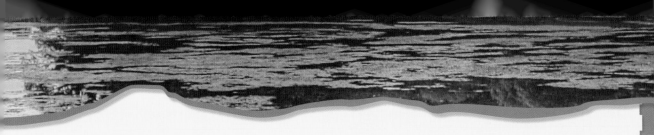

REPAIRING HABITATS

People can do a lot to help repair a damaged **habitat**. Picking up garbage in and around a river is one of the best ways to help. Another great way to help is to clear away **nonnative** plants in or near a river. This makes room for **native** plants to grow. Many groups also plant native shrubs and trees near riverbanks. These provide animals with food and homes. The roots from these plants also keep the riverbank from **eroding**.

KIDS MAKING A DIFFERENCE

Elementary school students at the Concord School in Windsor, Canada, have worked to repair the Little River **watershed** in their community. Since 1989 students have cleaned up tons of garbage from the Little River. They have also planted thousands of native trees and shrubs. Today, the area is a healthy **ecosystem** where plants and animals thrive.

Planting trees is a great way to help river habitats.

PROTECTING RIVERS

Some areas are protected by the government. A government may pass laws to protect a river or watershed from **pollution**. These laws prevent factories from dumping waste into rivers. In many areas, logging companies are not allowed to cut down trees. People are not allowed to hunt, fish, or gather plants there. Sometimes people are not allowed to camp or use motor vehicles in protected areas.

Some laws protect certain plants and animals that live in or around a river. All endangered species are protected by laws that prevent people from hunting them.

This sign shows that an area is reserved for protecting trout. People cannot fish them there.

Trout Habitat
PLEASE PROTECT YOUR WATERSHED
McMillan Creek Stewardship Group
56   500

TEACHING PEOPLE ABOUT RIVERS

Teaching people about river food chains and habitats is an important part of protecting them. People need to know what they can do to help river habitats. It is important to teach people who live near rivers to help rivers and not to hurt them. People who live near rivers can avoid planting nonnative plants. They can choose native plants instead. They can make sure not to take so many of the same kind of fish that they put the species at risk. Farmers can conserve (save) water and use natural **fertilizers** instead of chemicals.

SALMON IN THE CLASSROOM

Classrooms all over Washington state are raising baby salmon! Working with the Washington State Department of Fish and Wildlife, these classrooms each receive 500 salmon eggs. When the eggs hatch, the students care for the **fry**. Students learn about the salmon life cycle and about what salmon need to live. When the fry are big enough, the class goes on a field trip to release the salmon. The class sets them free in a local stream or river.

This student studies fish in their various stages of life.

TOP 10 THINGS YOU CAN DO TO PROTECT RIVERS

Even if you do not live near a river, your actions affect the rivers in your area. Even little changes can make a big difference! There are many ways kids can help rivers and river food chains. Here is a list of the top 10:

1 Never litter. Even litter on the streets can end up in rivers.

2 Encourage your family not to use **pesticides** on your lawn. Chemicals that go into sewers end up in rivers.

3 Try to use less **fossil fuel** (gasoline) to help stop **climate change**. That means walking or riding your bike instead of getting in the car. If it is too far to walk, consider carpooling or taking public transportation.

4 Only fish in designated areas and don't take fish that are **endangered**. Don't take more fish than you and your family can eat.

5 Write letters to people in government such as your state's governor, representatives, or even the president. Tell them why they should support laws that protect rivers and **watersheds**.

6 Volunteer to plant **native** trees and shrubs near a river or stream. Many communities have special tree-planting events.

7 Raise money for a **conservation** group. There are many ways kids can earn money. You could babysit, mow lawns, or have a garage sale.

8 Learn about plants and animals that live in rivers and tell people why they are at risk.

9 Talk to your teacher or youth group leader about getting involved in conservation work. Maybe your class can raise salmon, plant trees, or raise money to help an endangered **species**.

10 Pick up litter near a stream or river in your neighborhood. You can do this by yourself, with your family and friends, or with a group.

GLOSSARY

adapt change in a way that helps a living thing survive in its environment

adaptation special structures or behaviors that make an organism well suited to its environment

algae (singular: **alga**) simple, plantlike organisms

alien animal or plant that is brought by people to a new environment

bacteria (singular: **bacterium**) tiny living decomposers found everywhere

basin dip in the land

brackish freshwater mixed with salty water from the sea

carnivore animal that eats the flesh of other animals

climate weather conditions in an area

climate change human-made changes in weather patterns

conservation protecting and saving the natural environment

consumer organism that eats other organisms

contagious easily passed from one animal or person to another

current movement of water in a river or ocean

decomposer organism that breaks down and gets nutrients from dead plants and animals and their waste

echolocation locating objects by reflected sound

ecosystem community of plants and animals and the area in which they live

endangered at risk of dying out

energy power needed to grow, move, and live

eroding wearing away of rocks and soil by wind, water, ice, or chemicals

erosion when rocks and soil are worn away by wind, water, ice, or chemicals

estuary mouth of a river where freshwater mixes with water from the sea

extinct when all living things of a certain kind have died out

fertilizer chemical substance added to soil to make plants grow faster and bigger

fossil fuel fuel that comes from the remains of plants and animals that lived millions of years ago

fry young fish

fungi (singular: **fungus**) group of decomposer organisms including mushrooms, toadstools, and their relatives

habitat place where an organism lives

herbivore animal that eats plants

hydroelectricity electricity produced by the power of flowing water

irrigate supply an area with water, usually to grow crops

larvae (singular: **larva**) young of some insects and other animals

GLOSSARY

mammal warm-blooded animal that produces milk to feed its young

migrate to move from one area to another

mollusk soft-bodied animal, often with a hard shell, such as snails, mussels, and clams

native born, grown, or produced in a certain place

nitrate chemical that contains nitrogen

nonnative organism that was not born, grown, or produced in the area in which it now lives

nutrient chemical plants and animals need to live

omnivore animal that eats both plants and other animals

organic made in a natural way or containing only natural materials

organism any living thing

pesticide poisonous chemical used to kill insects and other pests

photosynthesis process plants use to turn energy from the Sun into food and oxygen

plankton drifting plants and animals

pollute release harmful waste into the land, air, or water

pollution harmful waste

predator animal that hunts another animal for food

prey animal that is hunted by another animal

primary consumer animal that eats plants

producer organism that can make its own food; a plant

scavenger organism that feeds on dead plant and animal material and waste

secondary consumer animal that eats primary consumers and other secondary consumers

silt fine particles of eroded rock and soil that can settle in lakes and rivers, sometimes blocking the movement of water

spawn produce young as eggs

species type of plant or animal

talons claws on birds of prey

tropical having to do with a region of high temperatures and heavy rainfall

watershed area of land that drains into a river system

wetland area of land that is covered with water, such as a swamp or marsh

FIND OUT MORE

BOOKS

Arnosky, Jim. *The Brook Book: Exploring the Smallest Streams.* New York: Dutton Children's Books, 2008.

Campbell, Andrew. *Wetlands in Danger* (*Protecting Habitats*). New York: Franklin Watts, 2008.

Chambers, Catherine, and Nicholas Lapthorn. *Rivers* (*Mapping Earthforms*). Chicago: Heinemann Library, 2008.

Johansson, Philip. *Lakes and Rivers: A Freshwater Web of Life.* Berkeley Heights, N.J.: Enslow, 2008.

Solway, Andrew. *Food Chains and Webs: The Struggle to Survive.* Vero Beach, Fla.: Rourke, 2009.

WEBSITES

www.internationalrivers.org
The website of the organization International Rivers offers more information about preserving rivers.

www.rivernetwork.org
The website of the River Network organization provides facts about rivers, as well as ideas for how you can get involved in saving rivers.

http://kids.nationalgeographic.com/Animals/CreatureFeature/River-otter
This National Geographic website for kids provides facts about the river otter.

www.ncsriverkids.org
At this River Kids website, learn how other kids are working to preserve rivers.

FURTHER RESEARCH

Choose a topic from this book you'd like to research further. Do you live near a river you would like to know more about? Or is there a faraway river you think is exotic? Was there a creature in this book you find interesting? Is there something harming river food chains you'd like to know more about putting a stop to? Visit your local library to find out more information.

INDEX